The Firefly And The Firewall

How I Taught Cybersecurity to my 7-Year-Old Twins!

Jwalitha Matangi

/ BookLeaf
Publishing

India | USA | UK

Made with ❤ on the BookLeaf Publishing Platform
www.bookleafpub.in
www.bookleafpub.com

Dedication

To all the children stepping into a world woven with the
digital,
may you explore it with curiosity, courage, and care.
And to my twins
you are the reason this journey began,
and the joy stitched into every line.

Preface

When my twins first asked what I do at work, I paused.
How could I explain "cybersecurity" to two seven-year-
olds whose world was painted with stories and crayons?
So, I began to speak their language — stories, rhythm,
and imagination. Between the hum of laptops and the
hush of lullabies, we created verses about passwords as
secret spells, data as hidden treasures, and firewalls as
magical shields.
What began as playful storytelling became a bridge
between my world of code and their world of wonder.
This book of poems, isn't just about cybersecurity — it's
about trust, awareness, and nurturing curiosity in a
digital age.
A mother's way of saying: *be kind, be curious, and
always click wisely.*

Acknowledgements

To my husband — for sharing every responsibility and
dream with such grace.
To my twins — my inspiration and joy in every line.
To my parents — for grounding me with love and
wisdom.
And to my friends — for their constant encouragement
and laughter along the way.

1. Dancing with Twins and Cyberspace

Is it easy to understand you?
No way — you're a riddle, just like my two!
Swapping secrets, trading grins,
Oh, what fun when the real play begins.

In cyberspace, the rules are new —
Do you click the thing that's bright and blue?
Should you chat with strangers or keep things tight?
Peek behind every digital light?
Well, everything's fun — or so it would seem,
But safety's the key in this glowing dream.

Once you learn it, you'll see it's true —
Cyberspace is twins — digital two!
Unlock the laughter, but stay secure,
Every click and giggle, pure.

**Life and the web — both rise and fall,
It's best when you're safe, and smiling through it all!**

2. The Cyber Garden we grew

Let's start with screens and remotes today,
What are we watching? Let's think, okay?
Before we play or scroll or view,
Let's make sure it's the right thing to do.
When you touch a phone or a game or site,
Can you click on everything in sight?
No, stop and ask an adult near,

They'll help you choose and keep things clear.
A stranger online may smile and chat,
But don't share photos or names like that.
Always ask before you send,
Adults help keep you safe, my friend.

In this cyber garden bright and true,
Safety grows in all we do.
Learning with care, me and you—
That's the cyber garden we grew.

3. Some pictures stay off Internet

I'd love to share your happy faces,
your smile, your fun, your favorite places,
But pictures tell more than we see—
they share your world, your identity.
So post with care, think twice, be smart,
keep some memories close to heart.
The internet never forgets its find,
so protect you—your face, your mind.

4. Why no screentime ?

You see your friends with glowing screens,
And wonder why I don't.
But little one, your time will come—
For now, I must say don't.
Your eyes are new to the world's bright light,
They need no restless glow.
Your mind's a garden, pure and fresh—
Too young for endless flow.
The world outside still waits for you,
With *sports, songs, and skies*—
There's magic more than screens can show,
Reflected in your eyes.

5. The Hero on the Screen!

When you watch a **hero** fly,
Or see them zoom across the sky—
Remember this, it's true, not fake:
You've got **power** too, when you're awake!

You share your games, your art, your smile,
You make the internet worthwhile.
But being safe is part of play,
So think before you click away.

Be **kind**, be **smart**, and take your time,
Don't fall for tricks or sneaky slime.

6. Be a Cyber Super Hero!

Don't click too fast, don't share too wide,
Keep your secrets safe inside.
Not every "friend" is who they say—
So think before you let them **play**.

Ask before you post or send,
Check with someone you trust, my friend.
Even if you're young and small,
Smart clicks help protect us all.

Cyber-safe means thinking clear,
And guarding all you hold so dear.
So when you're online, show you care—
Be a hero, everywhere!

7. My Secret Password!

You need a *password*, strong and neat,
To guard your data—what a feat!
A PIN as well, so none can peek,
At all the secrets that you keep.

Don't make it easy—no, no way!
Not your birthday or games you play.
Mix in letters, numbers too,
A puzzle that belongs to you!
Just like your face or fingerprint,

Your code's your shield—your safety hint.
Keep it safe and keep it tight,
Stay cyber smart, both day and night!

8. Twin's OTP Rule!

If someone asks for a little code,
That pops up on your phone — don't unload!
"Tell me the **OTP**," they beg and plea,
But hush — that secret is for *you* to keep.

If they stand outside or call when I'm not there,
Or say "It's from Mom" — stop and beware.
Don't give the numbers that flash on a screen,
Even if they say it's from Mom or Dad, or from
somewhere unseen.

So lock it up, don't type or say,
Tell a grown-up right away.
Hang up the phone, find someone near,
Keep your codes secret — loud and clear!

Keep it safe, keep it snug,
Your OTP's a little bug —
Hidden, private, just for you —
That's the smartest thing to do

9. Twins learning Deepfake with Aww!

"Look! That's me!"
Dancing in blue on the big screen!
But wait... I never danced at all!
How did my face get in that hall?
My friend said, "You're on the news!"
But my brain said, "Is this true?"
It looked so real, the sound was loud,
But something felt a little... wowed.

That's a **deepfake** — a sneaky trick!
It swaps your face super quick!
It makes fake voices, scenes, and sounds,
And spreads them fast all around!

Be safe, be smart, and always check,
Before you click or send that tech!

10. Mom, who's Alexa? And Siri too?

Twins: "They talk so nice — just like you!"
I laugh and smile, then softly say,
"They live inside our phones each day."
"They joke, they sing, they help us learn,
They tell the time — but can't discern.
They're made of code, not heart or grin,
No feelings live beneath their skin."

Me: "So never share your secrets, dear,
Like where we stay or who lives near.
They're smart and kind, but don't forget —
Real hearts are warmer yet!"
"So play and learn, explore with care,
Use tech with love and thought to spare.

**In this bright world of hum and fun —
Your voice, my children, is number one."**

11. AI and Me!

A robot friend or one that might bite?
I smile and say, "Not quite, my dear —
It's brains in wires, not snack or gear!"
It chats, it draws, it helps us play,

But sometimes gets our jokes halfway!
Just one rule, smart and cool,

Don't share what you wouldn't at school.
No names, no face, no secret place,

Keep your info in a safe-space case!
AI's a tool — clever and new,
But the boss of tech is **YOU!**

12. Hackers in the Screen!

Tap-tap-tap on a glowing screen,
Hackers hide like they're unseen.

Some protect and keep things right,
Some sneak around, out of sight.

Codes and keys are what they chase,
Cyber is their exploring place.

Be smart, be safe — as you explore,
Use your power to help, not score!

13. Aliens from the Sky!

Aliens fly with a cosmic zoom,
Across the stars — zoom-boom-boom!

Do they giggle? Do they shout?
We'll never know what they're about!

Curious creatures far from here,
The universe is theirs to steer.

We might think they're weird or new,
But they just want to learn like **you!**

14. Twins: A Bedtime Poem

It's bedtime, kids — come snuggle tight,
Our story glows in soft screen light.

No kings or queens on thrones so high,
Tonight, we code while fireflies fly!

No "once upon a time," I say,
But tales of clouds where data play.
Of robots kind and stars that gleam —
Still magic, just a different dream.
"Mom, are you police?" they asked one day,
"You chase bad people in your own way!

Some break the law — they're tracked and caught,
Cyber police protect a lot!"
"I'll be one too!" one of them, said with pride,
"To keep the world safe on the data side!"

15. The Computer Bully!

A bully hides inside the screen,
Quiet, sneaky — never seen.

It grabs your games and pictures too,
And says, "They stay... unless you do!"

It doesn't own your things, oh no!
It's just a mean pretend-friend foe.
So pause before you click or tap,
Some links are just a tricky trap!
If something strange pops up one day,
Call an adult right away.

Keep passwords strong and files backed up,
And that bully won't bother your stuff!

16. Stay Safe, Stay Cool!!

A stranger might smile and say,
"I have toys! Come play my way!"
But don't go with someone new —
They might trick and scare you too.
Stay with grown-ups that you know,
They'll keep safe the places you go.
If someone says, "Come here, come quick!"
Say **NO!** and move away real slick.
Hold a hand when in a crowd,
Don't wander far or call too loud.
If something feels weird — trust that feeling,
Run to help — no hiding, no dealing!
You're brave, you're smart — you won't be fooled,
You know the safety rules at school.
With family near and friends you trust,
The world is safe — and that's a must!

17. My Twins as Cyber Knights!

Mom, we've got stories bright and new,
With magic screens and gadgets too!

We're twin defenders—side by side,
Smart and brave with superhero pride!

We learn the clues, we spot the traps,
We keep safe keys from sneaky chaps.

Our capes are codes, our swords are brains,
We chase off villains with pixel flames!

Hand in hand, both strong and clever,
We guard the world—now and forever!

One day, Mom, you'll proudly say—
"My twins save worlds in their own way!"
New-age heroes, bold and true,
Cyber-knights — and they're just SEVEN too!

18. Assurance they need!

Long ago, my loves, you see,
Lived heroes brave as brave can be.
Dragons roared and giants cried,
But courage always turned the tide.

Kings and knights with hearts so true,
Fought for good—like you two do.
Dreams had wings, and magic shone,
In every tale I've ever known.

So when you dream, my dears,
Hold your courage, calm your fears.
For every age, in its own way,
Has heroes born each shining day

19. Dear Teacher, Teach Them Early...

The age of screens is here to stay,
Our little ones scroll, swipe, and play.

We hand a phone to calm their cries,
A tablet glowing in their eyes,
TV friends to make them smile,
Digital toys all the while.

Dear teacher, you light every mind,
With every lesson, kind by kind.
Could we add one more to start
Cyber safety from the heart?

Together we can pave the way,
Secure their future, day by day.
So, teach them early, guide them true,
Dear teacher, we believe in you

20. Pen Pals Then, Online Friends Now,,

Long ago, we had pen friends,
Who lived in places far away,
We wrote our names on pretty cards,
And waited for mail every day.
The postman came—Oh what a joy!
A letter just for me!
Stamps and stickers, secret notes,
Friends we couldn't see.

But now our messages blink and beep,
On phones and screens so bright,
New friends pop up and say "Hello!"
Morning, noon, and night.
Yet listen close, my smart young friend -
Be clever, brave, and strong!
Online or off, a friend is real
When they help you get along.

21. When Your Shining Eyes Ask Me!

When your bright eyes ask me,
"Where should I begin?"
I whisper, "Wonder is everywhere
Just take the first step in."

Learn from those who love you,
Their stories light the way.
Choose wisely on your glowing screen,
Let good things help you grow each day.

Books and worlds are waiting,
With secrets bold and new.
Stay safe, stay kind, protect each other
Let love be bright in you.

So keep exploring, little ones,
With courage, heart, and grace.
You'll help this world shine safer still
A better, loving place.